Contents

Handbook on Prayer
by Donna Steffen

Nihil Obstat
Rev. Msgr. Glenn D. Gardner, J.C.D.

Imprimatur
Most Rev. Charles V. Grahmann
Bishop of Dallas

April 2, 1999

The Nihil Obstat and Imprimatur are official declarations that the material reviewed is free of doctrinal or moral error. No implication is contained therein that those granting the Nihil Obstat and Imprimatur agree with the contents, opinions, or statements expressed.

Photos
© PhotoDisc, Inc., 4, 20, 32, 44; © Bill Wittman, 8; © Corbis/Digital Stock, 12, 24, 36; © Comstock, Inc. 1998, 16; © Ken Chernus/FPG International/PNI, 28; © Fabricius; Taylor/Stock, Boston/PNI, 40.

Send all inquiries to:
RCL • Resources for Christian Living
200 East Bethany Drive
Allen, Texas 75002-3804

Toll free   877-275-4725
Fax   800-688-8356

Visit us at www.rclweb.com

Printed in the United States of America

12724   ISBN 0-7829-0973-6

5 6 7 8 9 10 11 12

07 08 09 10 11 12

Introduction

*Y*ou have already set out on a faith journey.
Your faith is important to you and as it continues to
grow and develop, your relationship with God
becomes a more vital part of your life.

The human heart is drawn toward God. Our
spirits are satisfied with nothing less than God. The
psalmist's words, "Let me abide in your tent forever"
(Psalm 61:4) and "For God alone my soul waits in
silence" (Psalm 62:1), give voice to the human heart's
desire for God. Prayer becomes a means for this
union, this mingling of the heart with God.

Your relationship with God is nourished and
deepened through prayer, which is how we communicate with God, as well as through daily living. Just
as communication is essential—requiring time and
attention—in a relationship with a friend, parent,
child, or spouse, so it is in your relationship with
God. As with others, the more energy put into your
relationship with God, the more it will flourish.

Sometimes in your desire to grow in relationship
with God you may not always know how to develop
it. You may know only one way of praying, but
another way may be more helpful and enjoyable.
Perhaps your present way of praying is already satisfying, but you feel a desire to grow closer to God in
prayer. Let this desire—from the Spirit—lead you on.
Giving attention to your life of prayer, much as you
would tend to a garden, will facilitate the fullness
that is possible for you.

How you pray is also affected by a variety of
factors. Some people find relationships easy; others
find them a challenge. Some are able to open up

and trust another readily; for others, the path to a trusting relationship is slow. Some people enjoy reflecting and being quiet; others find it difficult to cease from activity and be alone with their thoughts. Because people are different, there is no single way of prayer that works for everyone. There is no right way or wrong way to pray. The best way for you to pray is the way that suits you, that's genuine.

This handbook examines various considerations that affect how you pray. These areas include your image of God, your ways of knowing yourself, the environment for your prayer, and your feelings and life concerns.

As you read these pages it is essential to reflect on your experiences. Take time to write your thoughts and insights in the spaces provided. Do not hurry through this book. Spend time praying and then reflecting on your prayer, even if you have only ten minutes a day. Take note of what moves your heart toward God. Prayer itself, not reading or thinking about it, is the best teacher.

With all that is known about prayer, there is no guaranteed way to grow in relationship with God. There are only guideposts. May these guideposts help you find your way more surely into the heart of God. Enjoy the journey ahead.

Begin this journey by examining your present prayer life. Reflect on your habit and experiences of prayer, and write your responses to the following:

Describe your present daily practice of prayer.

When, where, and how do you pray?

When you pray, do you: just talk to God, ask for something for yourself, pray for others, seek guidance, think things through, praise and thank God, or. . . ?

What do you like best about your prayer?

What are your questions or concerns about your prayer?

Imaging God

When I was a child, I used to think of God as the wind. When I would play outside or take walks I'd feel the wind on my face and know God was with me. When I'd see the trees move, I'd sense God was present. God was invisible like the wind. Yet I was assured of God's presence when I felt the wind or saw it moving branches or leaves.

Today, God is simply the God of my life, the one who created me and everything, and holds us all in love. Over the years I have always felt close to God. In recent years I have grown more steadily to trust God's ways.

Georgia Brucken

For Reflection

□ Recall your earliest memory of God. How old were you? What was God like for you then?

□ When you became a teenager and later a young adult, how did your view of God shift?

□ Describe what God is like for you now. Allow an image of God to arise in you. Sketch this image, or write the words that describe it. List six qualities that describe your God.

□ Now list any qualities of what you wish God was like for you.

&xploring images of God has become rather prevalent in various adult prayer and spirituality groups. People grow up thinking of God in a given way, and equate God with this particular image. The unlimited variety of images of God has been growing for centuries. For example, Catholic tradition provides images of the Trinitarian God who is Father, Son, and Spirit. Michelangelo's famous portrayal of God creating Adam provides a picture of God as an older man with white hair and a beard. Depictions of Jesus vary according to the culture in which he is portrayed. A dove, fire, and wind have been associated with the Holy Spirit.

Scripture includes numerous possibilities of what God is like. In the psalms God is likened to a shepherd (Psalms 23 and 80), a light (Psalm 27), and a rock (Psalms 18, 28, and 144). God is described as having hands (Psalms 91 and 98), and wings (Psalms 57 and 91). God is characterized as one who is loving and faithful (Psalms 25, 89, and 136), who gives shelter (Psalm 91), and who heals the brokenhearted (Psalm 147). Isaiah portrays a God likened to a mother who would not forget the child of her womb (Isaiah 49:15). The First Book of Kings describes God experienced in a gentle sound rather than in a strong wind, earthquake, or fire (1 Kings 19:11–13). These are only a few examples of the many rich images scripture provides.

All these images, revealing how people over the centuries have perceived God, may truly flavor your own images and experiences of God. A God who is like a rock may be strong and foundational, but simultaneously without warmth or tenderness. We might feel fearful before such a majestic God. Some classical categories of how God is perceived may include being close or distant, personal or impersonal, forgiving or unforgiving, compassionate or harsh.

People frequently confess, "I used to sense God as judging me, but now I have a loving God." This transition from an image of a predominantly judging God to a loving, forgiving God is not just a matter of pressing a button to change the way of thinking about God. Truly experiencing a loving God often requires the time to nurture a closer relationship with God. It involves gradually opening your entire life and very core to God in trust.

This relationship based on trust will mean absolute dependence on God, even when it is very difficult to be open to what God asks of us. Of course, if you knew in every fiber of your being how deeply God loves us, you would have no hesitation in letting go of your deepest attachments, even when "reason" tells you not to.

Your faith journey, then, requires that you acknowledge your honest feelings about God in all aspects of life. How do you experience God? What parts of your life are readily open to God in trust? What aspects of yourself do you hold back from God? And the answers to these questions depend on your dominant image of God.

Uncover your image of God by exploring:

- Images of God from childhood to the present.
- Qualities you experience in God.
- Your present feelings about God.
- How much of yourself you open to God.
- What part of yourself is held back from God.
- Thoughts, attitudes, and feelings you have about God.
- What draws you closer to God.
- What keeps you from growing closer to God.
- Your discoveries in a conversation with God.
- What more you want in your relationship with God.

Talking to God

Whenever I had a problem or needed some clarity about what to do, I would take time to pray and ask God's help to discover my answers. I would go over and over the situation in my mind. Then I would finally figure out what to do. It has only been a recent discovery that while I thought I was praying, I really spent most of my time thinking. I asked God's help, and then set out to find the solution. I had good intentions of letting God lead me. I found, though, that I asked God to help me find the way. This is different than letting God show me the direction. This discovery has set me on a whole new path with God. I'm excited about our new way of relating.

Melanie Strong

For Reflection

▦ Become aware of the process that happens in you as you pray. Notice how you begin, how you proceed, and what happens during your time of prayer. Place a percentage (20%, 50%, . . .) after each of the following to describe to what extent, when you pray, you are:

Aware of God's presence _____

Conscious that you are communicating with God _____

Allowing God to speak to you _____

Thinking about God_____

Thinking about a problem _____

Drifting off to the day's concerns _____

▦ Do you presently tell God about your feelings and experiences?

_____Sometimes

_____Always

_____Seldom

_____Never

▦ What are your present beliefs regarding telling God about your feelings and experiences?

*C*ommunication with God—prayer—happens in many ways. Specific ways of praying may help to deepen your relationship with God. Ordinary human relationships provide clues to the kinds of prayer that may enhance your union with God.

Friendship develops over time. Two people begin by talking about common interests. "I saw a great movie." "I enjoy concerts." Gradually they begin to express more of what is significant to them. "I'm having a hard time at work. My boss cuts into my turf. I get so angry." "I'm so excited about our new child. I never expected I'd have such a wonderful family." And then, over time, friends share even deeper parts of themselves. "I'm really struggling to find my way. On the surface, my family and job are fine. I'm just not sure who I am any more."

The level of sharing often moves from factual information, to expressing some relatively "safe" feelings, to disclosing more personal feelings. Self-disclosure involves a willingness to acknowledge and expose a deeper part of yourself, risking that the other will accept and love this true you.

Prayer involves similar considerations. How you pray depends on the degree you are willing to acknowledge your true self, and to what extent you are willing to be vulnerable to God.

Accepting your feelings is difficult, and expressing your feelings is even more so. Society promotes the opposite. We are told to "be good, be nice, put our best foot forward." When we feel anger, sadness, or disappointment, our habit is to put aside these feelings and "be nice." Men in particular are taught to hide certain feelings and not to cry. Each family teaches particular beliefs about expressing feelings. People sometimes apologize for tears, even at funerals. Confusion often occurs when more than one feeling is present. There may be gratitude for a past action, anger about something now, and we don't know what to do. The anger does not exclude the gratitude.

In prayer it is possible to keep God at a safe distance and share only surface parts of yourself. You might express facts more than feelings. Many people spend most of their prayer time praying for others. While this is important, it is also essential to pray about your own life, heart to heart, expressing your deepest feelings with God. One way to bring your own life into prayer is to tell God how you feel. "God, today I feel really discouraged. Yesterday when . . ." Sharing your experiences and feelings with God is quite different from being in God's presence and thinking about them. Some say, "But God already knows this." True. But knowing that your daughter won the science fair is different than hearing her tell you about it. When she does this, she is inviting you into dialogue with her, into a new level of relationship with her about her experience. The same with God.

When talking with God, take time to notice how connected you are with what you are saying. A lot of chatter happens in a day. When you pray, touch into your heart or inner self and talk there. It's a great gift whenever you are able to let God into your joy, weakness, tears, pain—into your heart.

Explore the "you" that relates to God by naming:

- ❀ Three feelings you often experience
- ❀ The feelings you like least
- ❀ Feelings you readily share with others
- ❀ Feelings you never share
- ❀ The person who knows the real you
- ❀ The feelings and experiences you share with God
- ❀ The part of you that you hide from God
- ❀ These explorations in prayer with God
- ❀ Your particular need of God's help with this
- ❀ Your prayer when connected with your heart and spirit

Praying for Your Desires

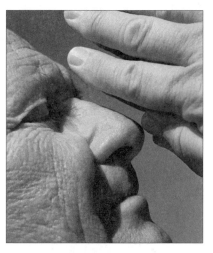

In my own heart I've had a secret longing to be closer to God. I've never told anyone this. Not even God. It's almost like I never had words for this longing before. Yet this longing is there. I've always felt a little odd or different. Do other people feel this way? No one talks about longing to be closer to God. I don't know what to do about it. Just putting words on this longing helps.

James Albright

For Reflection

 Make a list of all the things you desire. Just brainstorm them without judging them. Then circle the two or three desires that are most important for you.

 If you could ask God for something for yourself, what would it be? What does your heart want from God? What does your heart most want in your relationship with God?

 What is it like for you to think about what you desire?

*C*hristians as a rule are taught to put aside their desires, or at least to control them, to exert will power over them and be self-sacrificing. The Buddhist tradition teaches that people should let go of desire rather than give in to it, since fulfilling desire only breeds more desire.

The word "desire" brings up many associations. Our desires, part of our human makeup, are many and varied, as are our motives for them. People may connect desire primarily with lust or concupiscence. Someone may desire a new car just to have the latest model, or to have adequate means to get to work. Another may desire many material things to fill an emptiness, to gain prestige, to inflate their ego. We may desire a more satisfying marriage, more time to spend with children, or good health. An evening of good fun with friends may be our desire. The desire for a close relationship with God, "as the deer longs for flowing streams" (Psalm 42:1), may be the deepest longing of our heart.

Because we are created in God's image and are graced by God, we should be confident of our ability to desire what is truly good. To desire what makes us fully alive and truly loving of ourselves, of others, and of God is good. Some, many, of our desires fit this description. We forget that the greatest commandment includes healthy self-love, as well as love of God and neighbor (Matthew 22:36–40). Where we must be cautious is to distrust desires generally. This goes against deep spiritual truths that have long been part of our Christian tradition. Discernment is needed to distinguish our genuinely good desires from those that lead us away from our truest relationship with God and others. The deepest desires of the heart are found in the midst of all of our desires.

St. Ignatius Loyola (1491–1556) wrote his well-known Spiritual Exercises after his own conversion. In each of the prayer sessions, he instructs the person to pray for the particular grace—the desire—wanted from God. It is as if Ignatius sensed that God placed the desire in the human heart. But God, very respectful of us, does not barge in, uninvited. God waits for us to ask for what we desire, to pray for it, before acting. It's as if God has a fishing pole and puts out bait, waits for us to bite, and then reels us in. God places the desires of the heart within us.

Our heart's desires may include the desire for family needs, for an experience of God's presence, for repentance for some wrong done, for the willingness to forgive, for true self-knowledge. In asking God for what we want, several things are happening. There's an underlying belief that God hears us, cares for us, and wants to respond. Expressing our desires to God makes us vulnerable, and thus deepens our relationship. The practice of asking God for what we desire, noticing God's response or seeming lack of it, telling God how we feel about this, and repeating our prayer is to be deeply engaged in our spiritual journey. If we do this, we will not be disappointed.

Pray for what you desire by:

- ⊛ Naming your feelings and beliefs about your desires.
- ⊛ Writing the three deepest desires of your heart.
- ⊛ Bringing these desires to God in prayer.
- ⊛ Expressing your thoughts or beliefs about praying for your desires.
- ⊛ Telling God what you think or believe.
- ⊛ Noticing God's response or seeming lack of response.
- ⊛ Becoming aware of your feelings about God's response.
- ⊛ Telling God how you feel.
- ⊛ Asking for the grace you desire.
- ⊛ Continuing this practice often.

Letting God Speak

I talk to God a lot. I talk when I'm driving, as I walk from here to there, and as I do various tasks. I talk to God when I go into church or during Mass. What I find hard is listening. I find it difficult to quiet down and be still. I'm not very patient. Even with my family and friends I notice that when they begin to tell me something, I'm already thinking of how I'm going to respond. Listening is not my best suit.

Ericka Tasynski

For Reflection

□ Would you describe yourself as someone who is a good listener? Why or why not?

□ Name a recent time when you sensed that God spoke to you. In what ways did you experience God speaking?

□ When are you most apt to listen to God? When are you least disposed to listen to God?

*C*ommunicating with God in prayer involves not only talking to God but listening to God as well. Often people are better at talking. Some are skeptical as to whether God really speaks. God speaks in many ways: through the events of our lives, a song, nature, or in quiet prayer. And God speaks with a variety of nuances.

What does it mean to say that God speaks in a sunset, in the quiet of the winter trees, or in a mountain? Coming into the presence of nature in its simplicity and beauty brings us to a special place inside ourselves. Nature simply is what it is. In the presence of nature we encounter truth, humility, reality as it is and as we are. These qualities expose us to God's presence. When we are able to inhale the presence of God, away from our day-to-day distractions, we can hear interiorly. In nature's silence we come to know more surely our own voice, feelings, truth. Clarity comes. In nature's violent upheavals we may sense God's majesty and power. And whether we experience God's voice distinctly or not, there's a place inside us that knows we have encountered the sacred. We come home in heightened awareness of ourselves and of God.

God speaks through life's events. Often we experience a nudging inside to say or do something, or go somewhere, with no particular goal. Later, in looking back, we see how one event triggered another, which led to some experience God had orchestrated.

God may indeed speak through anything—songs, words on the side of a truck, a spiderweb, or the feel of spring grass on bare feet. Take note of the ways you experience God. Go back to them in prayer. Tell God about your experiences and thank God for them. Always notice when your heart is moved or something stirs in you. Become familiar with God's unique ways of communicating with you.

Scripture provides many instances of God's voice being heard. Abraham and Sarah heard God speak of a child that would be born and of a covenant with generations of people to come. Job, after shouting his prayer to God, heard God's response. Isaiah, Jeremiah, and Jonah heard God's call, described as if hearing a voice. Though not an audible voice, they heard or knew something inside themselves and knew it was of God.

The writings of scripture and of many saints, and perhaps your own experiences, indicate the possibility of hearing God speak to us directly. The prayer of listening requires a quieting down inside, a composure of mind; at times it also requires patient waiting, and always the trust that God will indeed respond. God's response is not automatic. Learning to listen takes time. A place within, however, will recognize the voice of God. Notice if there is a particular place in your body where you seem to sense God's voice, whether in your mind, your heart, or your abdomen. The way to this place is not always apparent, even for those who regularly practice listening prayer. The prayer of listening is worth the effort. The gift of hearing God speak inwardly is so wonderful that once it is experienced nothing less is satisfying.

Hear God's voice:

⚬ In nature.

⚬ In music.

⚬ In the events of your life.

⚬ In small coincidences you notice.

⚬ In a chapel.

⚬ In people.

⚬ In scripture.

⚬ In the quiet of your heart.

⚬ In a place inside your body.

Exploring Resistance

$\mathcal{S}$ometimes I wonder if I'm two different people. I really want to get closer to God. I often decide to take a few minutes after supper or just before I go to bed and pray. The time comes, and I find so many other things to do. When I do sit down to pray, my mind goes in many different directions. I feel frustrated. I can't seem to make the leap to prayer. Then I think that perhaps I'm already living as God wants me to, and I shouldn't worry about praying more. I should just accept this.

Gloria Martinez

For Reflection

☒ Become aware of your own patterns of avoiding prayer. List as many as you are able to. What feelings arise in you as you consider these?

☒ At what particular times did you consciously avoid praying? What were the reasons you chose not to pray?

☒ Become familiar with your "self talk," the things you tell yourself in your mind. What are some of the things you tell yourself about prayer when you aren't praying?

*R*esistance is the spiritual term for avoiding prayer. Everyone experiences it from time to time. Resistance is not bad. You might not even be aware that you are avoiding prayer.

Resistance to prayer is often a sign that there's some growth around the corner in your life, some new and deeper part of yourself that wants to emerge, some change coming on the horizon. Either consciously or unconsciously you resist this change, because change means some things will be different. Perhaps everything is not perfect the way it is, but at least it is familiar. Change may require something scary or difficult. Resistance emerges, then, as protection from the potential difficulty of change.

Let's look at two examples. Someone might resist praying in order not to admit to God some dissatisfaction with a job. While there is discontent, there are also good aspects, such as financial security and social opportunities. Yet the mere experience of dissatisfaction is discomforting. Things are no longer as good as they have been, and praying would mean facing facts and being truthful to God about these feelings.

Another person may sense that a relationship is no longer what it was. Still, the relationship could deepen as a result of working out the problems. This is not how it feels, though, and the fear keeps this person from acknowledging his or her true feelings. Prayer is resisted because the readiness to bring these honest feelings before God in prayer is not there.

Often resistance to prayer may not be obvious. Recognizing the resistance, becoming aware that you're not praying because there's something you don't really want to deal with, is a first step. The next step is not to overcome the resistance, but to respect it and get to know it.

Begin to understand why you are not praying. Perhaps there's an image that describes how the resistance feels, like confronting a brick wall, or something pressing upon your chest, or an emptiness. Then tell God about the resistance, the image of it, and the fear involved. Invite God to be with you in this. One thing is certain: God, who loves, has gentle ways, and is very patient, is on your side. God will wait as long as is needed for the readiness to come. Over time a willingness to look at what lies beneath the resistance emerges.

Resistance commonly manifests itself in several ways. We rationalize about why the feelings should be suppressed or why the present situation is acceptable. We use common spiritual clichés to keep real feelings at a distance. We intellectualize the situation in endlessly reading books on the subject. We may also use clever strategies to support our resistance to prayer, such as sleeping too much, overworking to keep busy, eating too much, or reading many novels. All of these serve to keep the true experience from coming to the surface. Bringing resistance and the deep fear to a loving God in prayer results, over time, in new life, and in a deeper, trusting relationship with God.

Remember that resistance:

- Is a normal part of prayer.
- Is a sign of movement occurring.
- Comes as a protection from the unknown.
- Might be conscious or unconscious.
- Is helped by being brought into awareness.
- Frequently has an image.
- Is often accompanied by fear of change.
- Needs to be befriended and respected.
- Can be shared with a gentle, loving God.
- Will move away when it is ready.

Preparing a Sacred Space

I have my own little ritual when I pray. I clear away any magazines or clutter around. Then I go to my prayer table and light the candle I bought just for my prayer. I breathe  and then bow with my hands together before God. I ask God to be with me. Then I sit and pray. Having my own place to pray has helped me feel God's presence. It's like a little chapel in my house.

Maria Corridino

For Reflection

☒ Picture your favorite places to pray. Describe each of them.

☒ Some people find it easy to pray in a church. What is it about a church that helps you pray?

☒ Often we have certain habits or rituals of prayer. What are your familiar ways of beginning or ending your prayer?

*T*he story goes that a novice in a religious community asked the Novice Director if she could knit while she prayed. The director replied, "No. When you pray, you must give your full attention to God." The next day the novice asked, "Is it okay if I pray while I knit?" The director said, "Yes. You can pray no matter what you are doing."

Of course, prayer can accompany any activity! Entering into prayer more deeply requires focusing attention on God. Often when praying at home other things make it difficult to concentrate. Work, phone calls, and endless little chores demand attention. Praying requires turning our attention away from all the busyness that surrounds us and focusing on God.

Serious preparation for prayer includes claiming time from a busy calendar and schedule. Some people actually write the time for their prayer on their calendar. Finding a time that will really work for you is helpful. If you hate to get up in the morning, or early morning is a hectic time at your house, then getting up fifteen minutes earlier each day to pray will likely result in failure and frustration. Choose what will actually work for you. Perhaps claiming twenty minutes twice a week on your calendar for yourself is more realistic. If you are a morning person, choose that time. If you are a night person, pray then. Whatever time you choose, the act of claiming it for your prayer gives a message to your whole being (and perhaps those around you) that you value your life of prayer.

Creating an environment of what suggests sacred space for yourself facilitates prayer. Creating a sacred space physically supports the inner desire to pray. Various items may enhance your prayer space. A small prayer table with an attractive cloth claims sacred space. Perhaps you might place a small meaningful object on the table, such as a stone found on a retreat, a picture of yourself as a child, a sea shell, or fresh flowers. Have a favorite copy of the Bible or a journal there. Lighting a candle helps to enter sacred space. The fragrance of incense may be useful. You might also support your prayer with soft, reflective background music. A fancy space is not the goal. Use what helps you pray. It might be nothing more than a cup of hot coffee in the morning.

Enter the sacred space within yourself as well. Find out what helps you touch your own heart and spirit, and bring yourself into contact with God. Taking several deep breaths, feeling the breath as it enters and leaves your body, might assist you in forgetting other things and becoming present to yourself. Listening to meditative music or looking at a candle flame may serve a similar purpose. Inviting God to be present or offering this time to God may be a suitable way to begin. Slowly reading a psalm that fits your present experience of God might help you enter this time of prayer.

Try what sounds appealing. Use what works. Discover what is best for you.

Create sacred space by:

⊛ Marking time on your calendar.

⊛ Designating a prayer table.

⊛ Using a symbolic object.

⊛ Playing soft music.

⊛ Burning incense.

⊛ Lighting a candle.

⊛ Wearing a prayer shawl.

⊛ Following your breathing.

⊛ Asking God to be present.

⊛ Giving yourself over to God.

Writing in a Journal

I went to a parish retreat. We were asked to bring a journal, or notebook, and write in it several times during the retreat. I've never liked to write, but this is a different experience. For about six months now I have been writing in my journal almost daily. Sometimes I write only a few sentences about all that's happening to me. More often I express how I'm feeling. Putting my thoughts in the journal has helped me be aware of myself in the midst of all the crazy busyness. What's been most surprising is that as I write, more comes out than I knew was inside. I sense God and I are doing this together.

Jerry Flaherty

For Reflection

▦ Think about the ways you use writing to express yourself to others: in letters, notes in greeting cards, memos on a kitchen board or at the office. What are the ways you communicate yourself to others in written form?

▦ When were times you wrote in a diary, wrote your reflections on an event for a newsletter, jotted down some ideas you wanted to remember, or wrote poetry?

▦ Become aware of your feelings about writing. In what ways has writing served you well, surprised you, inspired you, frightened you, or challenged you?

$\mathcal{G}$o to any bookstore and you will find a shelf on writing. There are the traditional forms of writing instructions, such as how to write a term paper or a newsletter. In recent years many books have been published on writing as private self-expression and as a way to creativity. This writing accesses not only the mind, but the heart, emotions, and what the unconscious self knows.

Writing daily in a journal helps to focus your own life when you are pulled in many different directions. Writing in the morning about your feelings as you begin the day connects you with the inner you that will live the day. Writing in the evening can help make you aware of the day's events that were significant, moving, upsetting, rewarding. Over time writing serves to keep you aware of the you that's living your life, without being swept away by life's demands.

Some people choose to write in a journal when strong emotions arise within them. For example, rather than blurting out anger at someone, expressing in writing how they feel helps let out some of the steam and clarify the details that provoked the anger. Usually any one strong emotion involves nuances of other feelings as well. These feelings may seem all muddled, over-whelming, or confusing, but by expressing them in writing some clarity about the inner experience may be achieved. When emotions are strong, it is easy to resist writing because of the energy needed to explore them and the discomfort that might be felt. However, those who engage in this practice find that unclouded thoughts and feelings are the reward. The release from the confusion and stress of the emotions is a benefit that outweighs the effort.

Taking a longer block of time to write is profitable. In this process of writing new insights and awareness unfold. Writing is a key to a deeper resource within the self. Often a revelation about one's self, another person, or a situation emerges from writing. Christian tradition teaches that God dwells within us (1 Corinthians 3:16). The process of writing taps into this wisdom. Taking this belief of God's indwelling seriously means that God is involved in all that is revealed through written self-expression. God is not "added on" to the writing, but is present in the process itself as an inroad to our deepest self. The writings of many saints witness to this truth.

You may choose to invite God to be present, and to lead, guide, and unfold whatever will be written. Others do all their writing as a letter to God, beginning each entry with "Dear God." Writing God a daily morning or evening letter, even brief, is a helpful practice of keeping in touch with yourself and your ongoing relationship with God. Writing keeps the mind from drifting and allows you to be entirely present. Though writing is not everyone's way, for many, many people it has been and is one of the most beneficial aids for the spiritual journey.

Writing Practices:

- Keep a journal or attractive book for your writing.
- Put your journal in a special place.
- Write your thoughts and feelings.
- Write a few minutes each morning and/or evening.
- Write a daily letter to God.
- Express your strong emotions in your journal.
- Explore childhood memories in writing.
- Write down dreams you remember.
- Describe how God speaks to you.
- Read over your writings periodically.
- Write until there's no more to write.

Using Formula Prayers

I find that I pray in different ways at different times. When I'm happy and light-hearted I like to sing hymns we use at church. Often the words and melody of psalm refrains run through my head. Sometimes I talk to God in my own words. When I'm tired or frustrated, I pray the rosary. It helps me feel connected with God. When I feel discouraged or depressed, I sometimes just finger the rosary beads. That's all I'm able to do and I find comfort. My own preferred prayer which I use over and over is simply "God, be with me." I almost always begin and end each day with a few of my favorite prayers.

Matthew Hurr

For Reflection

☒ Make a list of all of the prayers you have learned throughout your life. Include blessings at meal times, prayers before going to sleep, and prayers for special occasions. Which of these have you forgotten or ignored? Which prayers have become your favorite?

☒ Reflect on your prayer in the morning and evening, in a week's time, over a month. Which of these prayers do you use most frequently? At what times are you most likely to pray them?

☒ Think about your experience when praying these prayers. To what degree is your mind, heart, and spirit connected with these prayers? How often do they become rote, with your mind wandering elsewhere while you pray them? What is the effect of these prayers on your relationship with God?

$\mathcal{P}$raying with formulated, or fixed, prayers has always been part of the Church's tradition. The early Christians prayed the Lord's Prayer daily. Over time the Creeds, the Hail Mary, various prayers of the saints, the psalms, the rosary, and other formulas of prayer became helpful ways of praying. See the *Remembrance Book* (RCL, Foundations in Faith, 1998) for an extensive compilation of Catholic prayers.

The Lord's Prayer, recorded in the gospels of Matthew and Luke, is presented as Jesus' teaching about how to pray. The prayer arises in a heart that claims dependence on God for daily sustenance, and a willingness to ask for and offer forgiveness. Using plural pronouns, it has a communal dimension. The Church's liturgical prayer frequently incorporates the Lord's Prayer. Praying it daily aligns us with the prayer of fellow Christians.

The Hail Mary, whose formulation includes scripture from the annunciation and visitation, is part of the Church's rich tradition invoking Mary's intercession. It is incorporated into other forms of Marian prayer, including the Angelus and the rosary.

Trinitarian prayer also underpins the prayer of Catholic tradition. Liturgical prayer, as well as other gatherings of Catholics at prayer, frequently begins with the Sign of the Cross. We pray in the name of the persons of the Trinity, while we sign ourselves with the cross of Christ. We also conclude many prayers and psalms with the doxology, "Glory be . . . ," praising our Trinitarian God.

The rosary, a significant prayer of the Church, combines praying these foundational prayers, the Hail Mary and the Lord's Prayer, with reflection on scripture. The mysteries of faith of Mary's life as well as of Christ's life, death, and resurrection are used for reflection while the prayers are recited.

A prayer that simply repeats a word or phrase over and over is called a "mantra." The repetition of this prayer stills the mind and draws the heart's attention to God. It might be a sentence, such as "Give me a heart of love," or a single word, such as "peace." The individual pray-er may choose the words. The Jesus prayer, "Lord Jesus Christ, have mercy on me," given to a Russian peasant known only as a "pilgrim," is an example of a mantra, repeated silently or aloud over and over.

The psalms are a rich resource of formulated prayer. In recent years the sung psalm refrain at liturgy has served to make psalm verses part of many people's memories. Because the psalms embody a variety of prayers, they provide simple formula prayers, from longing, to praise, to contrition. The psalm refrain may be sung aloud or uttered within as a prayer.

Using any of these formulated prayers or other prayers from the saints offers a way of praying that is familiar, concrete, and helpful in many ways. These prayers draw our minds and hearts to God, integrating us into the larger prayer practice of the Church. They sustain us when our own words falter, they comfort us with their accustomed cadence, and they hearten us with a spiritual ambience.

Pray with formulated prayers:

- Make the Sign of the Cross.
- Pray the Lord's Prayer.
- Pray the Hail Mary.
- Pray the rosary while reflecting on the mysteries of faith.
- Use the Jesus prayer.
- Compose and pray a one-word mantra.
- Compose and pray a mantra that is a phrase.
- Sing a favorite psalm verse.
- Pray your cherished prayers each morning.
- Sing a hymn.

Praying with Scripture

The Bible used to seem like such a mammoth book to me. I never really understood it. A neighbor and I were talking once, and he gave me another way to look at the Bible. I now find God talking to me in the stories. It's like I'm right there, and Jesus speaks to me. Or I catch a glimpse of how Abraham and Sarah felt with God's promise to them. And the psalms. I love the psalms! I'm amazed at how incredibly human they are, and how often the prayers in them are my own. Why didn't someone tell me this sooner?

Kevin Taylor

For Reflection

 We have varied associations with the Bible, some are positive and some are negative. When you think of the Bible, what are some of your feelings?

 Think about your experience with the Bible.
Do you have a Bible? Is it a recent one or an older translation? What parts of the Bible have you read? Which parts of the Bible do you enjoy the most?

$\mathcal{P}$age through the Old Testament and look at the names of the various books. Which ones are familiar to you? Find the Book of Psalms and read a few of them. In the New Testament choose one of the gospels and read the headings of the events. Read one of the letters found after the gospels. What are your reflections about the scripture you read?

Scripture is a rich resource for prayer. God speaks through scripture not only to those at the time it was written, but to those who read it centuries later as well. Understanding all of the Bible is not necessary before using the parts that are helpful to you.

One real treasure in scripture is the Book of Psalms. The 150 psalms express prayer filled with a variety of human experiences. They include prayers of gratitude (Psalm 136), questioning (Psalm 10), longing (Psalm 13), love (Psalm 18), abandonment (Psalm 22), trust (Psalm 25), contrition (Psalm 51), and praise (Psalm 135). Choose a psalm that fits your heart today. Pray it slowly. Try reading it aloud as well. If one line seems to speak to you, pray only this one line. Let it dwell in your heart throughout the day. Psalms 23, 27, 34, and 139 are often favorites.

In recent years an early term in the Church's tradition of praying with scripture has been revived: Lectio Divina, or "divine reading." Choose a part of scripture for this prayer, possibly the gospel from the previous or coming Sunday, or a few paragraphs from one of Paul's letters. Become aware of God's presence, and invite God to lead you in prayer. Slowly read the scripture. After a moment of quiet, notice what word or phrase speaks to you. Read the scripture again. What is God saying to you? Respond to God with your heartfelt words. Read the scripture again. Rest with God without words, and then thank God for this time.

St. Ignatius of Loyola describes ways of meditating that give us two approaches to praying with scripture. Ignatian meditation uses the powers of memory, will, and intellect to sense the meaning of scripture for our lives. For example, Mark 4:35–41 tells the story of Jesus and his disciples in a boat while a storm arises. Meditating on this might involve reflecting on the storms in your own life. Hearing Jesus' questions about faith leads to applying the need for faith in those troubled areas. The prayer ends by asking God for faith and peace in the midst of the particular storms of life.

Ignatian contemplation also involves the use of our imagination. In this second form of prayer we enter the scene, feel emotions, and often personally encounter Jesus (when using the gospels). Using Mark 4:35–41, invite God to unfold the prayer. Read the passage and visualize the scene with the people and setting. Smell the smells, hear the sounds, feel the wind, and picture yourself there. You may be off to the side or become one of the apostles in the boat. Then let the scene unfold with feelings arising as conversation and actions occur, beyond what is recorded in scripture. For example, someone could become angry at Jesus' suggestion not to be afraid. Then let the dialogue with Jesus unfold. The prayer ends by expressing your heart's prayer to God.

Don't worry about the details of a particular method. Your own way of praying with scripture may be a combination of these descriptions.

When praying with scripture:

- ⦿ Choose a particular scripture passage for prayer.
- ⦿ Invite God to speak to you.
- ⦿ Come with anticipation of what God will say.
- ⦿ Read the scripture slowly, either aloud or silently.
- ⦿ Notice any particular words or phrases that speak to you.
- ⦿ Observe what moves your heart.
- ⦿ Be aware of your feelings as you pray.
- ⦿ Talk to God about what you hear.
- ⦿ Let your heart respond to God.
- ⦿ Rest quietly with God.
- ⦿ Hold these words of scripture within you throughout the day.

Centering Prayer and Contemplation

At one of my small group meetings, I was introduced to a way of praying that was totally new for me—centering prayer. We simply sat in silence, and let our minds quiet down. At first I thought this was really strange. We all just sat there so still. Someone coming in would have thought we were in a trance or something. I've come to like centering prayer. It seems to give me an anchor in my life. I begin each day with about twenty minutes of this prayer. It's like I have a solid foundation and I'm not easily pushed around. I'm so grateful to have found this way of praying.

Peter Rich

For Reflection

 Recall times you sat in the quiet of nature: next to a lake or stream, on a rock in the woods, or on a mountainside with a beautiful view. Think of times you sat gazing into a fire in a fireplace. Remember the effect this had on you. Write down your experience.

 Perhaps you have tried tai chi, yoga, or a meditation class at a health center. Maybe you are a swimmer or a long-distance runner. What is the effect of these experiences on your mind, heart, and spirit?

 What other kinds of experiences have you had that helps your mind quiet down and gives you a sense of peace and well-being?

*C*entering prayer is a prayer of quiet, which takes different forms. For some, the word "meditating" is used interchangeably with this form of silent prayer. It involves sitting in God's presence in silence, motionless, with the mind entirely at rest. This is the difficult part. Because our minds are by nature active, their attention tends to drift here and there. Having something to focus on, without attached ideas, helps to quiet, empty the mind, allowing us to simply "be" in God's presence.

Looking at the flame of a candle is one method of centering. Just gaze at the light. When your mind moves away to something else, become aware that this has happened, let the thought go, and return to gazing at the flame. Another point of focus often used is breathing. Follow your breath in and out. In doing this, attention is brought inside the self. As with the focus of the candle flame, when becoming aware that the mind has drifted away from breathing, let the thought go, and return to the focus.

The posture recommended for centering prayer is sitting with the spine somewhat erect. Picture a string of light coming in the top of the head and going straight down the spine. The goal is that this string of light have a clear, direct path. For centering prayer it is helpful to find something to support the body in this posture, rather than using muscles that tire in holding the body erect. Try sitting upright in a straight chair without leaning against its back, feet flat on the floor. Sitting on the floor on the edge of a pillow, with legs crossed, might work better for your body. Place your hands on your lap with palms up or down, or with your thumbs just touching.

Centering prayer has various benefits. An awareness of your mind's specific patterns may emerge. You might notice that your mind frequently worries about events on the horizon, or more often replays past experiences. You might find it hard to let go of these thoughts and just be. After prayer time, pray or write about these patterns in your journal. When experiencing an inner place of quiet, insights or images often arise. Simply letting go and being in God's presence with nothing to do or be generates a sense of peace, well-being, and inner harmony.

Saints have described a prayer of contemplation with several of the same elements. They sat quietly in God's presence and experienced union, without thoughts. This experience of quiet prayer in union with God was received as a gift from God, rather than something willed to occur. Whether or not you attain this same degree of union with God, sitting quietly in God's presence gives God space to enter.

Contemplation is part of our human experience. We contemplatively look at a newborn baby, snow, or trees. Parents contemplatively look at a child asleep in bed. No words are needed. Theologian Walter Burghardt has described contemplation as "a long loving look at the real" (Church, Winter 1989). In contemplation we become fully present to what is before us, and rest in its presence.

Develop your contemplative spirit:

- Gaze at a sleeping child.
- Hold your hand before you and lovingly see it.
- Sit quietly in God's presence.
- Find a comfortable, centered way to sit.
- Sit in centering prayer for ten minutes a day for a week.
- Describe your mental patterns.
- Follow your breathing periodically throughout the day.
- Eat an orange while being present only to the orange.
- Wash dishes as if it were the most important thing in your life. Keep your thoughts on the dishes.
- Go to a tai chi or yoga class.
- Walk a labyrinth.
- Listen to classical music while doing nothing else.
- Sketch a flower.
- Walk in the woods.

Praying through All of Life's Experiences

*J*ust *last week someone asked me how I pray. I had a hard time answering. I pray in so many ways. Some of them do not fit any traditional way of praying, yet I know that for me they are prayer. For example, sometimes I sit in a tub of hot water on a winter's night and burn a fragrant candle. This helps me be with God. At other times I whisper little thoughts to God, such as, "Thanks for the parking space," and I know God and I are together. Sometimes at night I lie on the floor and listen to soft music, and God is with me. Once I even got up and danced, I felt so moved. There's no limit to how I pray. I'm sure I'll discover even more ways of praying.*

Patricia Rider

For Reflection

▨ Brainstorm all the ways you pray. Include anything that brings you to an awareness of God's presence. What are some ways of praying that you think are uniquely yours?

▨ Think of the variety of prayer experiences you have had. Perhaps you've gone to a retreat or workshop where there were unfamiliar forms of prayer used. Out of all of the ways of praying introduced to you throughout your life, what kinds of prayer do you like the most?

▨ As you go through a day, write down all the times and ways you pray in that day. Become aware of the extent to which your life and prayer are intertwined.

$\mathcal{S}$cripture exhorts us to "pray without ceasing" (1 Thessalonians 5:17). No part of human life is intended to be separate from God; experiences ranging from travel to using a computer, to organizing projects belong to God's domain. Where feelings such as love, peace, and satisfaction, anger, hurt, and revenge take up residence, this is where God wants to be. God waits for an invitation, then finds an inroad that is unique and personal.

Prayer, then, will take on many and varied expressions interweaving with all of life's experiences. Discovering your personal prayer paths is a wonderful adventure. Try anything and everything. Hike in a forest, jog by an ocean or river, look at the still waters of a lake, or walk through a church, museum, or inner city to come in touch with God. Listen to the voices of the poor. Listen to the quiet or loud voice of your soul. Find what yields an open heart and a sense of connection. Be aware of what leads to an experience of God's absence, as well as of presence. Hear the many ways God speaks to you.

God speaks through dreams, too. Scripture gives many instances of God's communication through dreams. Through listening to the revelations in his dreams (Matthew 1:18–2:22), Joseph knew he should wed Mary, flee to Egypt, and when to return and by what route. The meaning of dreams is not always clear. Feelings in dreams usually express true feelings that the awake self does not want to admit. Writing dreams in a notebook and asking God to show their meaning indicate a willingness to listen.

Walk, sit, lie down, or dance as a way to enhance your prayer. Particular body postures express the prayer that is inside the heart. Bowing the head suggests humility or sorrow. Raising hands and arms expresses openness and praise. Kneeling communicates dependence and contrition. Lying face up invites a sense of resting in God. Dance the song of your heart to God.

Walk reflectively and ask God to guide your steps when you do not know the way. Embody your prayer in a way that works for you. Pray with your whole heart, soul, mind, and body.

Prayer is simple. It does not need to be done in a new or different way. Sincerely bring your true self, with all its frailties and blemishes, to God, who wants to be with the real you. God loves you as you are, with your shortcomings, gifts, and peculiarities. When you bring this real you to prayer, then God is able to get inside and act.

The culture around us rewards material acquisitions more than spiritual quests, and production more than reflection. The blessing of awakening more deeply to the life of relationship with God is great. May you be generous in your gift of self to God in prayer. May your heart's desire for God be fulfilled.

Pray always—Pray all ways:

- Sit quietly and listen.
- Share your feelings of love and of anger.
- Speak about your experiences.
- Listen to God in the poor.
- Dance your song to God.
- Discover God speaking in your dreams.
- Sing your heart's song to God.
- Run or jog with God.
- Rest in God's presence.
- Sketch a picture of God and you.
- Be yourself with God.
- Whisper to God throughout the day.
- Let God accompany you when driving.
- Claim time and space to express your heart's desire for God.

Suggested Resources

Bacovcin, Helen, trans. *The Way of a Pilgrim* and *The Pilgrim Continues His Way*. Garden City, N.Y.: Image Books, 1978.

Barry, William, S.J. *God and You: Prayer as a Personal Relationship*. New York: Paulist Press, 1987.

_____. *God's Passionate Desire and Our Response*. Notre Dame, Ind.: Ave Maria Press, 1993.

_____. *Paying Attention to God: Discernment in Prayer*. Notre Dame, Ind.: Ave Maria Press, 1990.

Gura, Carol, et. al. *Remembrance Book*, Foundations in Faith Series. Allen, Tex.: RCL, 1998.

Hanh, Thich Nhat. *The Miracle of Mindfulness: A Manual on Meditation*. Boston: Beacon Press, 1987.

Huggett, Joyce. *Learning the Language of Prayer*. New York: Crossroad, 1997.

Keating, Thomas. *Invitation to Love*. New York: Continuum, 1997.

_____. *Open Mind, Open Heart: The Contemplative Dimension of the Gospel*. New York: Continuum, 1997.

May, Gerald. *The Awakened Heart: Opening Yourself to the Love You Need*. San Francisco: Harper & Row, 1991.

Merton, Thomas. *Contemplative Prayer*. Garden City, N.Y.: Image Books, 1971.

Nouwen, Henri. *With Open Hands*. Notre Dame, Ind.: Ave Maria Press, 1995.

Oliver, Mary. *New and Selected Poems*. Boston: Beacon Press, 1992.

Sheldrake, Philip, S.J. *Befriending Our Desires*. Notre Dame, Ind.: Ave Maria Press, 1994.